North and South Nodes

Guideposts of the Spirit

Cynthia Bohannon

ISBN-10: 0-86690-622-3
ISBN-13: 978-0-86690-622-7

Cover Design: Jack Cipolla

Published by:
American Federation of Astrologers, Inc.
6535 S. Rural Road
Tempe, AZ 85283

www.astrologers.com

Printed in the United States of America

Contents

Preface   vii

Understanding the Development of the Soul and Spirit   1

The North and South Nodes   7

North Node in the Signs   11

North Node in the Houses   15

North Node Conjunct the Planets   19

North Node Conjunct Uranus in the Signs   23

North Node Conjunct Neptune in the Signs   27

North Node Conjunct the Moon and Neptune in the Signs   33

North Node Conjunct Pluto in the Signs   37

South Node in the Signs   41

South Node in the Houses   47

South Node Conjunct the Planets   53

South Node Conjunct Saturn in the Signs   57

South Node Conjunct Uranus in the Signs   61

South Node Conjunct Neptune in the Signs   65

South Node Conjunct Pluto in the Signs   69

South Node Conjunct Lilith in the Signs   75

Transiting Planets Conjunct the Natal South Node   81

Saturn-Uranus Conjunction in the Houses   85

Appendix, Dealing with Emotions   91

Dedication

This book was written by the twin spirits, Ovensy and Lester, who have given us this divine gift of love from God. It is their contribution to the great spiritual science of astrology for the time had come for this information to be known.

My special thanks and love to Ted George, a most unselfish, spiritual and devoted astrologer who recorded the spiritual sessions and assembled the material for publication. Without him, this book would not have been possible.

We dedicate this book to present and future astrologers everywhere.

Preface

Because of the many prejudices against the science of astrology by scientists, religious groups, government, and others, investigation of this vast science has fallen to the individual astrologer for the most part. Thus there is a lack of necessary financial resources to conduct large scale scientific studies into every facet of astrology.

Governments pour millions of dollars into research programs that are of no practical use except to a few, but funds for astrological research are unavailable. The fact that there is any research being conducted at all is a tribute to those dedicated individuals and organizations who carryon their own investigations using their own resources. They know it is the greatest of all sciences, and its value has been proven over and over again, but to prove it to the skeptics and the prejudiced at the scientific level would require resources far beyond their capabilities.

Astrology persists and grows because of its own merits and in spite of its antagonists. It will continue to grow and expand as we enter the New Age. Research must continue and it must expand in order that a proper base of truth be established for the generation to follow.

How then can a proper base be established for the next generation when there is this lack of resources? The alternative is psychic research oriented to astrology. It can be carried on at very little cost, and it provides a high level of truth not otherwise available to earthly beings. Through telepathic channels, discoveries have been made that could not be possible through other means. The result has been the emergence of an entirely new field of astrology—spiritual astrology—through which truths have been brought out that were never before known.

It was through psychic research that the author was able to bring forth the astounding interpretations of the nodal placements contained in this book.

This vital research must continue so that astrology will become an accurate and precise field of study for all that wish to use it. Its vastness is something to behold, and for earthly beings to do it justice in this age Age seems impossible, but it can at least be investigated and research pursued in those areas of most importance to the majority.

The future course of mankind depends on it.

Ted George

Chapter 1

Understanding the Development
of the Soul and Spirit

The soul is a separate entity from the spirit, and it is the main body force in each of us. It is located just outside of the material body, just slightly above the head region. The spirit is a product of the soul created by a combination of soul and spirit forces, and it is located within each individual. Earth beings will soon learn to distinguish the two through particular devices scientists will one day be able to produce. The differences between the soul and the spirit are only slightly beyond the reach of conscious Earth beings.

The soul is the giver of life to the spirit, and it is the spirit which possesses those traits which we call the human being. The spirit and the soul are one with each other only at a particular point in time; that is, at the time of the incarnation. The incarnation occurs because of a choice made by the soul and the spirit entity which wishes to be developed. It is the soul that is the motivating factor behind the spirit, and the spirit is the force which is allowed to be creative and to develop at its own pace. The spirit is separated from the soul at a point in time, through what is called death, and the spirit continues to develop on its own. The soul is also left at this point in time to continue to develop on its own. It is as though there is a separating of the way between the two.

The soul is as a mother to the child. The child is given life by the mother, and the child develops through its own developing standards. The difference between the soul and the spirit is vast. The soul is a member of God's choir, so to speak. The choir of life through the soul is then brought down to earth and it is given to a particular entity to be developed, the entity called the spirit. The soul is the life giver to the spirit. The soul is a guiding factor in the life of the spirit, but after the incarnation is ended, the spirit is left on its own to develop at its own pace. The soul, which comes from God is the guiding factor in all creational events. It is the soul that is the true deeming factor behind the determination as to whether the spirit entity will begin its development or not. Also, the soul is very much influenced by the will of God, for God is the main energy source behind life for He is the true giver of life.

Now the soul is not exactly a separate entity from the spirit. To further explain, the soul is the father of life, and the spirit is the child of life. The difference between the soul and the spirit is that there is not always a true union between the two. The spirit is the energy source of life which is given the ability to develop through the help of the soul. Another example of a true energy source is known to us as God. The soul is to the spirit as a mother is to a child. The soul is continually in contact with the spirit entity until that time when it is allowed to separate from the spirit entity, at which time it returns to its former position within the choir of God.

The spirit is then left to continue its search for creativity and its union with God. The spirit is the entity which must learn to function by itself, and continue its creative growth. By creative growth, it is meant spiritual and physical growth. The spirit is never an entity that is dissipated into the ethers. The spirit is made by God, and is and will be forever and ever, as the soul is of God and it will be of God forever.

The soul is the entity that returns to each incarnation, and is therefore the one which returns to its original destination, which is with God. Actually, the soul does not really reincarnate. The soul is the entity which is the producer of the spirit, and the spirit lives within many planes at one time. The planes are vast and cover many learnings experiences for the spirit entity to become creative; that is, a creative process of God. The soul is the provider of life to this creative process. By creative process, it is meant dealing with life on the earthly plane, for the spirit creates the environment which surrounds it. It can be said that the environment within which we live is a figment of the imagination. We are are the makers or creators of our own existence.

At the completion of the incarnation, the spirit is not lost. The spirit is only living on the Earth plane in a very small framework of time. The earthly plane is only a small portion of the total environments within which Earthly beings presently exist. The spirit is separated from the soul at the time mutually agreed upon. This separation occurs when it is best for the spirit entity to continue on its own course. There is no particular "best" time to separate.

Those who have temporarily "died" but were revived have experienced the process of the spirit leaving the physical body. They describe their passing through a "tunnel" which in reality are the black holes in space as described by our scientists. The black holes are in the outer limits of our environment, and are not there to develop the spirit entities in any way. They are there to help develop an alternate energy source for the spirit entities living on this plane, and are there as a source of energy when the spirit entities separate from the soul. The black holes serve a dual purpose; that is, they are used by spirits to enter another realm of their creative process, and as an energy source for the spirits to draw from. In addition, they are there to help guide those who have lost their way from one plane of existence to another. It is a focal point for spirits, but many still do not find their way through to the other plane.

There may be several spirit guides to help develop the creative process of the individual entity after leaving this plane, and there may be others whom the entity may have known on the Earth plane. However, there are only a chosen few who are with the spirit entity by God's wishes to direct it to the proper area or proper resting area, whichever they deem fit.

An earthbound spirit chooses to be so because it no longer desires to continue on its chosen path. These spirits know that they are not truly one with God at that moment and are confused. They are constantly in, search of their true identity and they deem it best to look back to their last existence to uncover their fateful decision to be an earthbound entity. They are there by their own choosing, and they do not truly understand why they chose this existence. They do not wish tq separate from the last incarnation, and many feel they have somehow let God down, and themselves, by not being what they felt they should have been in their last incarnation. They are considered dead by both planes, and considered lost because they refuse to continue their journey towards the Central Force, that which is God. The entities that become Earthbound spirits are very much alone with themselves, being trapped within their particular environment, and never knowing the true light of God.

The soul is always of God's likeness, and only the spirit is fallible. It is up to the soul to guide the individual spirit entity through the lifetime; therefore, if the soul has failed in its position to help guide the spirit properly, the soul must work that partricular lesson :over again that it was trying to instill upon the spirit entity at the time of the previous incarnation. This is what is commonly referred to as karma.

The soul is a gift from God to benefit the individual spirit which is to become one with God ultimately. The soul never guides the spirit to commit crimes or evil things for the soul is of God and only God is the one who chooses whether an individual entity shall survive or die. That is to say, the soul is never in a position to influence an individual to commit suicide or other such things. The spirit can be influenced by many sources. These sources can be Earthbound entities who hang around the individual influencing the decisions of the spint. The soul always stays pure as it comes from God, for only the soul, which is of God, will be like God throughout eternity.

It is very important for the individual to learn to control his own destiny within this plane of existence. Only the individual entity has difficulty with the problems that await it on this particular plane. Therefore, the spirit has been given the soul as a guiding factor to help it in its early years of birth, so to speak. It will be left on its own at a later time to turn towards itself. If the soul has not guided the individual spirit properly, it has helped to create an entity that will have a very difficult time with its entire learning and creative process. The spirit entity will have difficulty learning the lessons it did not learn while in this plane of existence.

The soul that was chosen to guide the spirit entity known as Jesus of Nazareth was a very advanced soul, for this soul would have had many years of experiences in learning to place individuals within their right frame of existence. This would be a soul that would have much experience helping others and it would, therefore, be considered a very advanced soul as opposed to the soul who has had lesser lessons prior to its teaching experience are lesser souls. They are all of God. It is just that some are more experienced than others, and they will be the ones that God will call on first to handle a very difficult or a very special incarnation.

The soul and spirit enter the body together, but separately, through an area of the head known as the "fontanelles," and are there to help guide the energy source through the being which is to receive the light from God. They are always together for no being can be born without a soul and spirit. They do not enter the I body at the time of conception, but only when the body, has reached completion of development which is justl prior to birth. Therefore, abortion that may occur any time prior does not kill a human being. In the case of abortion, the spirit entity has chosen not to enter into this incarnation, therefore, the soul has also not incarnated. The soul has chosen to incarnate at another time. The guiding spirits of earth beings have much to do with the decision of the individual to have an abortion. They have a great influence over the individual they are guiding in this lifetime.

Chapter 2

North and South Nodes

The Nodes are important as they are there to help the spirit prior to entering the incarnation. They are for the benefit of the spirit and for the benefit of its spirit guides while the spirit entity is on the earth plane. The Nodes are not for the benefit of the soul and therefore are not involved in karma. The Nodes enable the spirit to look closer at the life as it is coming to be prior to entering the Earth plane, and they act as a resting place for the spirit. It is a decision of the spirit to deliberate once more before entering the incarnation, and thus gives the spirit an opportunity to pre-judge the life as it is going to be.

The Nodes in the signs point out to the spirit the major areas of health problems and concerns, and the best attributes of health as they will be located in the chart. The North Node is helpful to the spirit to deal with those areas of concern that may not be beneficial healthwise. The South Node is there to warn the spirit that there will be areas of the life that will be affected by this placement. The South Node does not always affect the health, but it does show the areas of concern to the spirit. The spirit will therefore know that this is a weak area of its existence when on the Earth plane.

The purpose of the Nodes is to help the spirit in this lifetime by giving the individual spirit a starting point to focus upon. They help the individual become oriented toward the initial goals which were undertaken prior to emerging on this plane of existence.

Each individual has free will, and the gift of the Nodes was given to be worked with as each individual wishes. One may use the gifts to benefit the lives of others, or they may not wish to use them in this way. In either case, everyone will be expected to account for their accomplishments while on the Earth plane. Everyone should work with both Nodes, as the tendency is to stay with the easiest influences in the life. All have certain obstacles to overcome, which is the method by which we grow and learn. It is the overcoming of the obstacles and the development of the individual that life is all about.

The Nodes are a key to the chart and are indicators of what will show up in the rest of the chart. The North Node is very much like the South Node in that they both work together to form a union. They may be related to the Eastern philosophy of Yin and Yang, the positive and the negative, as it takes both to make a whole in this realm of existence. The North Node is not entirely positive; neither is the South Node entirely negative.

The North Node is a gift of God to each spirit to be used as it deems best. It does not mean that it will be used properly even though the spirit chose the placement to be used wisely while it is on the Earth plane. It represents the area of confidence to the individual, and it is therefore likely to be taken for granted. Through free will it may also bring overindulgence and extreme behavior in those areas of the sign and house placements.

The South Node represents a lack of confidence and fear in the area of the sign and house placement, but most individual spirit entities choose to develop these areas. This allows them to overcome their lack of confidence thereby properly utilizing both their South and North Node configurations.

The South Node represents the lessons that are to be learned. If they are learned in a constructive and positive manner, great benefits will result. If the lessons to be learned are ignored, suffering will be the result. Each soul knows that the Nodes are the guiding points for the spirit's lifetime on earth. The Nodes work together, and they will always be there as a reminder of the purpose for the life. There must be obstacles to overcome, but all should learn to incorporate the obstacles into a constructive frame by putting the Nodal placements into a confident and working capacity. Those who have achieved this are the well-adjusted individuals on the earth plane.

The Nodes in Intercepted Signs: The effect of the Nodes is lessened when placed in intercepted signs. However, the Nodes are a gift of God, and therefore, they will always have an influence. The influence of the sign will be less, but it still affects the life.

The Aspects of the Nodes: The only permissible aspect to the Nodes is the conjunction, and the degrees of the conjunction are not to be considered. A conjunction occurs when a Node is in the same sign as a planet.

The Nodes in Transit: The Nodes affect the Solstice Points by transit. As they touch off a planetary placement in the chart, look to the Solstice Point for major affects. It must be an exact conjunction to the Solstice Point as they only work in this way. No other aspects are to be considered.

Important: Before proceeding with the delineation of charts, it would be most beneficial to read this entire book in order that there be a fuller understanding of the action of the Nodes in all areas of the chart. In this way, each delineation will have a fuller impact when applied to the chart.

> *"I come to enter your real world from my more real world in the higher vibrations. My world is real, so you see that dreams can come true because they are true in my dimension. Cling fast to dreams. Share with those in the spirit realms for they are future realities."*—The Spirit of Neptune

* * * * *

> *"There is a difference between angels and spirits. Angels have not incarnated and spirits have incarnated. However, spirits do achieve extremely high levels on a plane similar to that of angels. Angels are part of the Trinity, and it is, therefore, not necessary for them to incarnate. Some who were thought to have been angels in biblical history were in reality spirits on a very high level. Spirits guide—angels can alter events. Spirits do not interefere—angels have the power, with approval of God, to change events for the betterment of mankind. It is angels that cause miracles to occur. Spirits are not involved in such things as 'parting the Red Sea', for this is altering the natural sequence of the sea."*—The Spirit of Orthrocar

Chapter 3

North Node in the Signs

Aries

These individuals have great versatility, energy, and initiative with those things involving the sign and house. They are interested in all matters relating to the head which could also include the development of their phychic ability. It is also a good placement for one who wishes to be involved in a leadership capacity. Therefore, it would be good for leaders of those areas that require great initiative and energy, such as politics. They would thus be using their South Node in Libra and overcoming their lack of confidence with the public. The best house position for this placement would be the third, which would enhance the individual's communication ability.

Taurus

This would show one who enjoys indulgences in such matters as beauty, money, material possessions and all those things of a Taurean nature. It is a good placement for one who creates something for its beauty such as a fine cabinet. The best house placement for this configuration would be the seventh, as this would denote the acquisition of material possessions for the benefit of the rest of society.

Gemini

This is the verbal communicator and these people are happy with constant communication. They take great joy in continually expressing themselves, but they are also very good at listening when not speaking. It would be best to have this placement in the third house so that the individual would not only be a good speaker but would also excel in writing.

Cancer

These are persons who are very much wrapped up in their own emotions, but it would be good for those who wish to communicate their emotions to others. For example, they would be good at consoling another or at mothering others. They are helpful to those confined to the home for they also tend to spend much time in the home. These persons enjoy being in the company of women, and aiding those who seek to relieve the plight of women in this society. They are the ones who enjoy growing things and like to bring happiness to others through their cooking skill. The best house position would be the fifth because they would love children and help them survive upon this Earth plane.

Leo

These are people who express themselves through words of love. These persons are the very gracious hearts of the universe, and have been given this gift in order to help bring the gift of love to Earth. This is the greatest gift of all—the gift of love from God. It can also be those who spend their time in the pursuit of happiness, which would include entertainment and physical pleasures. But the most important aspect of this position is thoughts of love. The eleventh house would be a good position for it would encourage these people to show love to humanity.

Virgo

There is a great capacity for helping others and an interest in healing by those with this placement. These individuals get pleasure in worrying over others they are helping. They have been given the gift of healing and serving others, but they are not necessarily completely consumed in their work. The sixth would be the best house placement as they would help others who are less fortunate and who need a helping hand from those that enjoy giving it.

Libra

Here is an excellent placement, for it spreads love and compassion to others. They wish to show harmony and equality to the world, and it can also be those who spread the inspiration of music to others. These are people who wish to have a happy partnership, but do not necessarily have a happy partnership. They do, however, continually seek the ideal partner, but do not find what they seek because of their high ideals and love of harmonious situations. Having this placement in Spica would give these people the ability to love others as well as themselves. The best house would be the seventh for it would spread harmony to the world.

Scorpio

This is very good for investigative pursuits such as scientific research and areas of the occult. They can spend hours with those things that others find very tedious. They have the ever-searching minds to continually work in these fields. This configuration gives enjoyment of sexual pleasures, but it does not necessarily give a fulfilling sex life. The person would constantly search for new sexual areas to explore, but may never truly achieve a completely fulfilling sexual relationship. They have a great interest in the world of the dead, but may not benefit from it. The best house would be the first because the start of any research must emanate from the mind.

Sagittarius

This is a very good placement for the development of the spiritual, and the spiritual is the best gift of God. It is given to those who truly deserve this gift, and who are being rewarded. They are here to help spread the spiritual word of God to others. The best house is the third of communication for it would enable them to express themselves as great spiritual teachers.

Capricorn

These people wish to help the less fortunate. They enjoy poverty and pursue those things involving the poor. They may be poor themselves, but they are still helpful to those who live in poverty-stricken areas. They are able to understand what is necessary to help the less fortunate and minorities. These are also the individuals who may be concerned about poor living conditions even if they are not actually involved. They are the ones who say that slum areas should be cleaned up, but do nothing about it. They are, however, happy to help others who are less fortunate than themselves. The less honest would be those who enjoy taking money for the poor but not necessarily using it to help them. The third would be the best house placement as it would enable them to educate the less fortunate in helping themselves.

Aquarius

This is not as strange as it may appear to be. These persons enjoy helping humanity at any cost. They express concern for the world through strange outlets, but do express themselves in some way to benefit all. They have an interest in astrology and it is a way for them to communicate humanitarian ideals to others. The best house is the seventh as the person would bring humanity to the public where it needs to be. The tenth house would also be good for it could bring humanitarian leaders of governments who would respond to the needs of the less fortunate.

Pisces

This is a good position for it brings happiness to those who are suffering. They are the ones who need the comfort of this configuration, and they enjoy helping others to help themselves, and are the great helpers of the less fortunate. They are indulgent in helping those who are ill. They could be quite indulgent in those things ruled by this sign, and they do get into trouble over their mischievous deeds. This configuration would be good in the sixth house of healing and service, for these things are needed most by the ill and the unfortunate.

Chapter 4

North Node in the Houses

First House

This is a good position for one who wishes to initiate things. These people are always great leaders in some way, including government, business, religion, and other areas of society. They continually search for outlets to put their leadership talents to good use. They should be encouraged to initiate and lead as they shine best when doing so.

Second House

Individuals with this placement constantly seek money and material wealth and discuss finances and new methods to make money. They are the great bankers and accountants as they have an aptitude for figures.

Third House

These are the constant communicators, looking for an outlet to express themselves, looking for someone to listen. They should incorporate their South Node placement in order to develop their spirituality. This serves a dual purpose in that it allow them to communicate spirituality and thus alleviate the negative areas of the South Node.

Fourth House

These are the complainers about their own situations. They enjoy staying at home, and should learn to find outlets other than the home, but also find work that will enable them to stay around the home base. They look for anything interesting related to women, real estate, agriculture, and the other areas of this house. They are the mothers of the universe, and it is therefore a good placement for motherhood. They should be guided to work outside of the home which would give them an additional, non-domestic outlet of expression.

Fifth House

These people are idealistic about love and the affairs of this house. They search for the perfect lover, and are often in love with love. They should be directed to investigate realistic matters such as those connected with the opposite house. Astrology would be a good outlet for them, as would the development of lasting friendships.

Sixth House

This is the constant worrier. These people truly enjoy worrying over trivial matters. They are the constant complainers about world conditions, and anything else they wish to worry over. Working with the less fortunate would allow them to concentrate their anxieties into constructive channels.

Seventh House

These are individuals who are continually involved with a partner and the public. They are lecturers or great politicians as they enjoy working with the public and being involved with public affairs. This placement is good for communicating truth, and these people inform others of that which they find to be truth. They should be guided to work with others who are less informed or are misinformed as this is the house of harmony and balance and there is a constant search for the proper perspective on life in general.

Eighth House

Here is a good placement for occult studies and for all matters of the dead. These people are constantly involved with the affairs of the dead, and often truly enjoy attending funerals. They look for something to stimulate their interest, and they therefore become involved with matters of the flesh. This can cause harm to another if poorly aspected. Since they enjoy intrigue, they could become destructive. These are the unusual thinkers who can be directed negatively to harm others, or directed to searching out the matters of the spiritual plane.

Ninth House

This is good for communicating spiritual matters to others. These people continually search for a true meaning to life, and become great philosophers as a result of this search. They look to others for guidance in other areas in order that they may explore the realm of the spirit world. They have a gift for teaching once they overcome their fear of speaking.

Tenth House

These people should work with the poor or in some high position in government. Great leaders of our time have this configuration. They have the power and ego to handle this placement, but they tend to complain about the unfortunate conditions of the world and should be guided to work in governmental matters or with the less fortunate. However, work with the less fortunate would be better because they could overdo their involvement in government. This, then, can be the gullible politician who becomes corrupt when given the opportunity. Used correctly, it could be a government social worker who truly enjoys helping the poor and unfortunate.

Eleventh House

These are the friendliest individuals. They truly enjoy friends and organizations and work well with both. They are good organizers and should learn to channel these energies constructively as they are prone to becoming too involved with their own hopes and wishes. If this placement is not properly handled, they can use their friends to their own benefit.

Twelfth House

These individuals enjoy indulgences and the vices of the world. They enjoy being in a state of intoxication or in a state of illusion while on drugs. They can be either destructive or extremely beneficial to others, and are frequently involved with those things relating to hospitals and other institutions. If this position is appropriately aspected, they can be excellent psychics.

> *"It is always helpful to send loving thoughts and healing energies to those in distress. The most effective way to transmit healing energy is by sending LOVE. It is important to know there are universal laws concerning healing with which one must become familiar if one wishes to practice this. Knowing the laws and how to apply them is very essential. Faith is necessary. Illness is a wonderful opportunity to discover and apply the laws of self-healing, but it is often perceived in a negative way by the person who is ill. We stress that everyone bless their illness and use it as an opportunity for growth."*—The Spirit of Poul

Chapter 5

North Node Conjunct the Planets

Sun

This gives great vitality in those things ruled by the sign and house, and these individuals can be very indulgent in these areas. For example, in Leo, these are people who indulge in love affairs, pleasures, entertainment, or sports.

Venus

These people are inclined toward social pursuits. It is a good configuration for financial and physical pleasures, and these people are generally very physical in their activities.

Mercury

This is a good placement for communication as well as travel, which these people have a tendency to overdo. They can communicate with the spiritual if they work with their South Node placement. If not, they would seek the spiritual but never truly accept it. They should be guided to choose a particular spiritual path to follow rather than constantly seeking out new areas of spiritual understanding.

Moon

These people are is inclined to be emotional in the areas represented by the sign place-ment. Working with the South Node placement can eliminate the emotional effects of the Moon. These individuals would do well to work with the less fortunate, as they would be incorporating their South Node configuration, thereby helping to eliminate the emotional stress connected with this placement. There is a tendency to over-indulge with the North Node placement, wherever it is located.

Saturn

This is an unfortunate position as it takes away the pleasures of the North Node, which are a gift of God. It therefore becomes a problem to overcome rather than a gift. These people are those who have forfeited the gift and therefore bring on their own sorrows. Many of the sorrows can be alleviated by working with the South Node placement.

Jupiter

This indicates extreme over-indulgence in the sign and house placements. It brings money to these areas and other benefits as denoted by the planet. These areas can be so easy to handle that they can bring extra problems connected with the South Node posi-tion. Through neglect of the South Node, misfortune arises. This can easily be overcome.

Mars

These individuals are tempermental with the associated sign and house areas, and place a lot of emphasis on these things, with frequent arguments and conflict. They actually enjoy arguments connected with this placement. Accidents are minor and can bring about rewards from such sources as insurance money if placed in the appropriate house.

Uranus

This indicates erratic and unusual behavior connected with the sign placement, which brings unhappiness at times. These people enjoy sudden changes and thereby ignore the South Node placement. It can thus bring misfortune because of a lack of attention to the opposite area. They do enjoy the scientific and unusual side of life.

Neptune

These are inspired individuals who also inspire others, particularly in creative areas. They also are creative. When used improperly, these people are very deceptive.

Pluto

Here is a powerful configuration as it brings psychic awareness to these individuals. They can work very well for the benefit of other people. Properly placed, they would enjoy affairs of the dead and would be great psychics for the public. Negatively, they can become involved with the underworld.

Vulcan

This is a very good position for healing as these people have an affinity for helping others. The individuals should be encouraged to work for others in whatever capacity they undertake.•

Persephone

This denotes creative ability as well as musical ability, but there is a tendency to over-indulge in these areas. Those individuals who inporporate the South Node placement with this would be very creative and use it for the betterment of society. They spread good will and inspire others to humanitarian goals.

Locating Vulcan and Persephone in the Chart

Vulcan is a child of the Moon, and its sign placement is either in the same sign as the natal Moon, in the sign preceding or the one following. It was discovered in 1977, and named Chiron, and it rules the sign Virgo.

Persephone does not have a regular motion. It travels between Mercury, the Sun, Venus and Jupiter, taking between sixteen and forty-two days to complete an orbit through a sign, and sixty days when in retrograde potion. Persephone will be a maximum of sixty degrees from the natal Sun placement.

"Each and every spirit has a particular task to perform at all times. There are those who are capable of being able to have responsibility for more than one task at a time, much like what is experienced at work. There are also those who have the ability to accomplish a great deal of work without much effort at all. And there are those who are seemingly busy constantly but who never accomplish anything. In relation to the spirit world, it is like one who is constantly striving to find the answer to a particular problem, but who is always heading off in the wrong direction. Direction is of great importance in the lives of those on the earth plane as well as those on the spiritual plane."—The Spirit of Ephraim

Chapter 6

North Node Conjunct Uranus in the Signs

Aries

There are unusual beginnings for those with this placement. They are erratic in their leadership ability and in beginning new projects. There is an unusual lifetime due to this placement. These people should work for organizations that allow them to use their creativity. Their erratic behavior can be overcome through the use of the opposite Node. This position is similar to the conjunction of the South Node to Uranus, but the difference here is that this position is more beneficial.

Taurus

This indicates creative endeavors with a touch of the unusual. There are unusual ways of earning money, and these people work to advance their material wealth. They receive lessons from others that will help to eliminate worry over financial problems. The lessons come via Uranus, for this is a very giving placement. Those connected with individuals who have this placement benefit from the unusual generosity of these people. Giving brings out the better side of both nodal placements.

Gemini

Here is the unusual and erratic communicator. These people constantly seek to gain attention for their communication ability. Some are great impersonators who use this means to call attention to themselves. They could do well in the field of comedy if this placement indicates such a career.

Cancer

These individuals generally have an unusual mother. They have an affinity for women and like to communicate with women through astrology as well as food and domestic life. There will be those who have a fear of unusual women, and others who are attracted to the unusual women of the world, depending on other placements affecting this sign. The South Node conjunction Uranus in Cancer brings a fear of unusual women, and this placement brings an attraction to unusual women. There is a fondness for the mother as well as for women in general.

Leo

This is very good for working with unusual children, especially those who are very receptive to spiritual communication. Many of these people work for the benefit of all, and they have good communication ability in spiritual affairs.

Virgo

These peoople should work with the less fortunate, either through the use of astrology or through technological advancements. This is very good for healing and a good placement for physicians as there is an affinity for the health profession in general. They are concerned about the future and are therefore given the gift of the scientific when used properly. Improperly used, this indicates those who work for the less fortunate for their own gain and benefit. They are the people who use this gift of God selfishly by seeking monetary gain to enhance their own material wealth.

Libra

These people have a gift for helping the public, and they can be exceptional politicians in government or other areas of society. They can be great influencers of public opinion when this placement is used constructively. There is an attraction to an unusual partner or one who is psychically inclined. Also, there is an inclination for all of the Libra professions, but the most beneficial use would be working for the benefit of the public.

Scorpio

These people can do well working with the occult sciences as they have technical as well as occult ability, and thus can benefit from both. They will be the founders within a structure that will initiate the beginning of spirituality, and can overcome their lower side by working for the advancement of all in their efforts to prove the existence of the spiritual plane. Used negatively, they would use their psychic abilities for their own advancement and material gain.

Sagittarius

This brings the unusual philosopher or professor of philosophy, and unusual individuals in general. They are the ones who constantly change their opinions regarding philosophical answers to the problems of the world. These people should work not only with the teaching side of their nature but also with the spiritual side. Once they have overcome their erratic behavior, they will do best with the world of the spiritual.

Capricorn

These are the unusual political leaders within government, and they should stay within the technical side of their career rather than the administrative side. They will work for the benefit of the less fortunate through the use of technology and astrology, but because their way of doing things is so unusual, they can have a difficult time expressing this to others.

Aquarius

This denotes a very scattered and erratic individual. However, these persons enjoy their erratic behavior and express themselves in this way. They should apply their genius to the scientific and to astrology, which will help them to overcome their scattered tendencies. Concerned about the world situation, they work to its benefit once they properly channel their genius.

Pisces

This brings the unusual psychic as well as the unusual skeptic due to the fact that they are fearful of that which is received spiritually. They should be encouraged to overcome the fear of the unknown, and would benefit greatly from working with the less fortunate as this would help them overcome their fears. These people enjoy hiding behind their fears. They do have a tendency to be attracted to unusual drugs, and should stay away from them. Inclined to over-indulge in unusual things that come their way, they would benefit most channeling their psychic ability constructively in order to overcome their fear of life.

Chapter 8

North Node Conjunct Neptune in the Signs

Aries

This brings inspirational leadership ability, and these people enjoy working with the spiritual as well as the occult sciences. They would do well to channel their creative energies toward these endeavors as they are the thinkers as well as leaders if they allow themselves to be so. Working with the South Node can bring direction into their lives. These people must channel their energies properly; otherwise, they will meet the wrath of the negative side of Neptune's influence. They should work with the leadership of the world in some form.

Taurus

This is a very creative placement, and these people should work with their hands because they enjoy building and constructing things. They should work with the creative side of Neptune's influence. Working with the receptive side of Neptune would inspire them to be devious with money and financial matters. They should work with the South Node in Scorpio and help others through their gift of intuition. Working with the less fortunate would help them to develop their creative abilities. These persons can be the psychic artists who receive messages from the spirit world and transfer them to paper or canvas. Using this position constructively rather than deceptively will bring these persons the best benefits.

Gemini

Here is the very devious speaker or the very inspirational teacher. They should use the positive side of Neptune, thereby incorporating the inspiration they can pass on to children, and by working with their South Node to bring spirituality to all through their teaching. Negatively used, these people would be good at deceiving others through their speech, writing, or other forms of communication.

Cancer

These individuals are either involved with deceptive women or very inspiring women. They should be careful to work with the positive side of Neptune as this will help to overcome their involvements with devious and deceptive women. A woman with this placement can be quite devious. This can be overcome if she inspires her children. It will benefit these people to work with the less fortunate in some way, thereby utilizing their South Node placement in Capricorn as this would be most beneficial for their development.

Leo

This represents inspired love affairs and inspired leadership. These people should work for the benefit of children, but if the inspiration is not channeled properly, it can denote those who would bring harm to children. They persons can be truly inspired by children, particularly those who are psychically gifted. These people should work with their South Node in the sign of organizations, which can overcome the negative tendencies of this placement., as well as with gifted children, some of whom will develop strong psychic ability.

Virgo

These people should work with disease or health organizations, and they will be involved with all types of sorrow as they are concerned with helping others in order to help themselves. The South Node placement can be easily incorporated with this position for they have the positive influence of Neptune in addition to the lesser influence of the South Node placement. These placements work well together to bring out the higher and the lower emphasis of Neptune. They can be inspired by work and can inspire employees.

Libra

This represents inspired, harmonious endeavors. They do best bringing harmony to the public and would do well with involvement in this area. These people should ilitilize their South Node placement of leadership in order that they can bring leadership as well as love of the public. They would also benefit through the creative side of their nature, thereby bringing out the positive side of Neptune. The negative side of Neptune brings deception of the public and partner. They can be inspired through deceiving the public if they do not channel their energies correctly. In either case, they would enjoy involvement with the public.

Scorpio

This is an ideal placement for those who wish to be invblved with the occult. They have been given this gift to work with it in a constructive manner, and if they choose to use it negatively, they will eventually reap its wrath. They should help the less fortunate, but they are very easily influenced by the lower side of Scorpio as well as the lower side of Neptune. Working with their South Node placement can bring more creativity and love to their spiritual studies, thereby bringing out the positive and constructive side of this position. These people are intrigued with death and the affairs of the dead, or the deceptive areas relating to the underworld. They should avoid such areas as this powerful placement can be used for destruction as well as constructive purposes.

Sagittarius

These people can inspire others to discover the spiritual world and the philosophic realms, and generally inspire others. Some will become world religious leaders. They should work with their South Node placement of communication in order to share their spiritual experiences with others. This is a powerful conjunction in whatever way it is used, and these people are God's helpers whether they realize it or not. This is a great gift, and these people can be greatly rewarded if it is used properly.

Capricorn

This is a good position for working with the disadvantaged and less fortunate. These people can be inspirational or devious. They should incorporate their South Node placement in order to overcome their lack of confidence in the home by working with others who have a home life that is much worse than their own. These people have been given the gift of helping and serving others who are less fortunate and they should use this gift in this manner. They can be inspired by farming and would do well to help the less fortunate through their talents in tilling the soil.

Aquarius

These are inspiring but erratic individuals who are endowed with two very powerful influences that will have a very pronounced affect on their lives. They are unusually psychic and these psychic gifts will come to them in very strange and unusual forms. By using their South Node placement they will learn to love those who come to them for help. They would do well in the scientific field, thus combining the psychic with the scientific, and can be instrumental in reconstructing the world for the future.

Pisces

This is a very good position when used positively. These people can be over-indulgent, or they can be very spiritual psychics. In either case, they will always be involved with the less fortunate as they are propelled into this area in some way. Thus they will use their South Node in the sign of service. Negatively, these are the people who over-indulge in some area. They can be inspired to work with the negative side of this placement, but the best benefits come through helping and serving others.

> *"I was an unusual phenomena for my time on earth. I was a negro physician. I am the one who discovered the process of separating plasma so that it could be stored for future use when needed for transfusions.*

> *"Though my discovery has helped save many lives, this was not the thing that resulted in the elevation of my soul. Helping others is of great importance and elevates the soul to some extent, but it was my death that elevated me spiritually.*

"I was critically wounded in an automobile accident and had lost a great deal of blood. I was taken to the nearest hospital, but I was refused admittance because it was a white hospital and I was colored. Therefore, I was denied the life-saving process that I had discovered. I died before I could be taken to a colored hospital.

"The message I bring is that the elevation of the soul into a higher spiritual plane resulted in forgetting that wrong which had been done to me. This is what is required by all. This not only involves the mental process of intellectual understanding as why events occur as they do, but the understanding which must also come from the heart. "—The Spirit of Charles Drew

Chapter 9

North Node Conjunct the Moon
and Neptune in the Signs

This placement is interesting in that it brings an unusual personality to the individual. The North Node brings a higher elevation to the placement of the Moon, and in general gives the person an optimistic outlook on life.

These positions are given to the individuals as a reward for benefits they earned in a prior existence. They have suffered before and God has given them this blessing as a way of honoring their past achievements. These people will do well wherever they place their energies, and it is good to know them for they will bring goodness to everyone in their sphere of influence.

The placement of the North Node with the Moon-Neptune conjunction brings only trivial ailments to these individuals so that most will not have to worry about health matters. However, the reverse is true when the South Node is conjunct Neptune or conjunct the Moon and Neptune. The South Node is a difficult position and represents particular obstacles that the individual must learn to deal with in order to overcome them. They are given the strength to overcome the obstacles through the inspiration of God and the help of Neptune. They would do well to work with the spiritual throughout their lifetime.

Aries

This placement brings much happiness to the soul as the Moon and Neptune work very well together, particularly in the area of the North Node. It influences these people to work toward a positive, soul-searching endeavor which can help to elevate the soul. These people help many who are less fortunate as this is an inspirational position. When worked with properly, they are the leaders of good causes. They should learn to work for the good of the public for it will help to overcome their lack of confidence as indicated by the South Node in the sign of the public.

Taurus

This brings wealth to the individual when used in a constructive manner. These people are creative and can bring beauty and happiness to their soul as well as to others. This position brings inspiration to their creative abilities, and they can do well working with women in a creative area or in the areas of the occult or sexuality. They can be inspiring teachers that benefit many.

Gemini

These people are inspired teachers, and the best area for them to teach is the spiritual because then they would also be working with their South Node. They can be an inspiration to others who know little of the spiritual world, and some are great teachers of the universe.

Cancer

This brings the great souls who are sent to Earth to help the unfortunate children of the world. They bring happiness to others by helping the less fortunate, and are blessed by the gift of motherhood and helping those who need them the most.

Leo

These are the leaders of the world. They are the ever-loving hearts who are here to help humanity, and have a natural desire to do so. These people bring happiness to everyone who comes in contact with them, and they will help many who are less fortunate than themselves.

Virgo

These people are very good at helping others with their health problems, and they do well in any position they choose as they have been given this gift to help others. They will serve humanity in some way, such as healing and serving others in an inspired way.

Libra

This is a good placement for partners and the public. These people can do well working with unions that have not already been corrupted. They are the inspired public officials, or those that inspire the public if they overcome their fear of leadership. Here to serve, they have the good of the people in mind and do well working with the public.

Scorpio

These are the good psychics and occultists as they have a natural feel for this area and have been given the gift of helping others through the benefits of the psychic mind. They should incorporate their South Node placement as well and overcome their lack of confidence in the creative side of their nature. Many will benefit from their knowledge of the spiritual world as these persons are naturally attuned to this plane of consciousness.

Sagittarius

Any area of the spiritual world would be good for these people. Given the gift of bringing spirituality to others, they should work with the South Node placement by teaching and writing about what they know of the spiritual. They are the messengers of God, and can carry out a heavy karmic burden in helping those who most need it. Although they may have a heavy cross to bear, the rewards will be beyond belief.

Capricorn

These people can be great farmers, for they will have the knowledge of the soil to grow crops no matter how difficult the conditions. They will work for the good of all by helping to bring food to those who need it. Thus they will incorporate their South Node placement in the sign of agriculture. There may be a desperate need of food during this transit period, and these people will work with those who are less fortunate.

Aquarius

Astrology is a natural for these individuals, who can bring many benefits to others through their use of it. Doing this, they can incorporate their South Node placement of love by learning to love humanity. These persons will have electrical as well as mechanical abilities and will be of great benefit to society. They are inspired by these abilities and will always use them properly. It is of great importance, however, that they work with their South Node placement, or this great gift will be lost.

Pisces

These individuals are truly spiritual psychics as they have the deep intuitive power of Neptune as well as the gift of Pisces to bring out the benefits of that which God has given them. These positions work well together as the Moon and Neptune are good for inspiring others. They should work in a service capacity for their South Node placement gives them a lack of confidence in work. However, they are able to work well with the spiritual, thereby combining the South Node and North Node placements.

Chapter 10

North Node Conjunct Pluto in the Signs

Aries

These individuals have powerful leadership abilities and a great aptitude of the mind. They can be great psychics if they work constructively with this placement. Thus they can be great leaders as well as great psychics and therefore benefit many. They should involve themselves with the South Node in order to overcome their fear of the public, thereby bringing their leadership abilities to the masses.

Taurus

People with this configuration are great teachers in creative fields. Their best benefits come through helping the less fortunate for they would then use the power of Pluto and the love of Taurus. They make great lovers for they truly appreciate the world through their creative endeavors. By working with their South Node placement, they can overcome their fear of the occult and the lower elements of society. They can bring great love to the lesser elements when this placement is properly used as they do have a love for all humanity. Given the gift of creativity, they will benefit a great deal if they work within this area. When this position is used negatively, it can be the over-indulgent, materialistic individual.

Gemini

This brings powerful and creative teachers when properly used. They have a gift for psychic writing and the occult, and can become automatic writers as well as great teachers. By using their South Node placement in teaching the spiritual, they can greatly benefit their lives. They should listen to their inner thoughts because they are actually communication from the spirit world. Having the gift of psychic ability, they should be encouraged to work in this area.

Cancer

Females with this placement are leaders and can become very prominant as well as very powerful, thus bringing great things to the world when this placement is properly used. They should be encouraged to work with the less fortunate, especially women as they have been given the greatest gift of love, which should be spread to all. These people truly love the benefits that Pluto brings. This placement can apply to men in the same way through aiding the women of the world and the less fortunate.

Leo

This is the great leader and the great lover. They have a heart of gold and will do many things for their society. They will learn to love humanity whether they wish to or not because they are here to guide and help whenever they can. This may manifest itself in an unusual way if they work positively with their South Node. They will accomplish many things for children and the other areas of Leo in general.

Virgo

Here is an interesting position in that it brings the psychic physician as well as the psychic healer. They work with their psychic ability whether they realize it or not. These people have the power of healing through touch, and can be very useful by learning to help the less fortunate people of the world. They should work within the health profession as it increases their ability to heal others, and they should also work within the area of the occult to strengthen their psychic awareness and healing powers.

Libra

This is good for creative endeavors and these people can do well working with the public, which can help them overcome their fear of leadership as indicated by the South Node. They will have a powerful influence over the public if they use these placements well. Their leadership can calm many, and bring humor and creativity to those who suffer, and they will be blessed by God for helping the less fortunate in this manner.

Scorpio

This is a powerful placement. It brings the great psychics who can read minds and work in any field of endeavor. They are required to work with their psychic ability, or the benefits of Pluto will backfire on them and the lower side will manifest, bringing difficulties and harm. By incorporating the South Node in the sign of love, they can overcome any negativity that may occur.

Sagittarius

This is a very interesting configuration for it brings powerful spiritual leaders when they are most needed. Many will be in a great need for spiritual rejuvenation when this position comes into focus, and these people will inspire others as well as themselves. By incorporating their South Node placement, they will spread the spiritual through the gift of teaching. This is a powerful spiritual position.

Capricorn

This is a good position for political pursuits as these persons do well working within the government because they can bring benefits to all when this placement is properly used. They should also work with the less fortunate as they will have a very strong influence over disadvatnaged people in their society. By using the South Node placement, they will become sympathetic, humanitarian, and compassionate leaders. If they disregard it, a wrath will be bestowed upon them that they will never forget.

Aquarius

This placement that brings interesting results because it can be associated with great scientific minds, spiritual and occult leaders, and great astrologer when properly used.

These people can have a great influence on humanity in the Age of Aquarius, and should learn to use their South Node placement in the sign of love to promote the benefits of humanity. They are truly blessed by God, and many will work to bring wonderful and beneficial things to the human race.

Pisces

This placement is good for spiritual pursuits as well as working with the less fortunate. They should work with the South Node to bring healing as well as spiritual and psychic pursuits to the the masses. They are very good people when they properly channel their nodal placements. Those who use this negatively, however, choose the lower side of life. Some who use this energy well become great human beings that benefit all who come in contact with them.

Chapter 11

South Node in the Signs

The most difficult signs for the South Node are Aries, Virgo, and Libra, in that order. In Aries, the individual lacks the ability for spiritual communication and it creates many false starts in life. In Virgo, it affects the general health of the person, and in Libra, imbalance within the person's system. However, in all cases, the fears and lack of confidence associated with the South Node can be overcome by using the Nodes together in a positive manner.

It must be remembered that although the Nodes can denote illness in the area of the signs, the person must still look for other indicators in the chart as to the strength of the illness. The illness could be latent, or the illness could be minor if it did not show up strongly elsewhere in the chart.

Aries

This denotes those who have a difficult time with their start in life. There are problems relating to the environment through many false starts in the associated areas of this house, and there is difficulty in completing projects and in developing communication with the spiritual plane. These people are prone to problems involving the head and face that can show up intermittently throughout the lifetime.

Taurus

This brings difficulties with material possessions. It does not necessarily mean that these people are deprived of the material things of life, but it does give them the feeling that they have not accumulated enough of what they need. This can bring health problems related to the throat area, pituitary gland, thyroid, and other glands located near this area.

Gemini

There are problems with communication and it is troublesome for those who wish to write. These people are less involved with relatives for they often feel uncomfortable associating with them. The lack of confidence in these areas can be overcome by working with the North Node placement, which will bring relief through spiritual awareness for the benefit of others. These people can be great communicators, bringing spiritual truths to the public. This placement can bring health problems connected with the nervous system and the parts of the human anatomy related to this sign.

Cancer

There is a lack of confidence in home life, and a tendency for these people to throw themselves into their work, thus avoiding home and personal involvement with women. Women have a great influence in their lives, which can help them overcome a fear of women. These people have an affinity for women as well as mother figures, and would do well to fight for women's rights. This is a good configuration for working with women who are less fortunate, or for working closely with female associates and thus utilizing the North Node placement. There can be a problem related to the health of a woman or one related to the female organs or other parts of the body ruled by this sign.

Leo

This is difficult for love affairs, men, and working with children. These people should work with their North Node in Aquarius, which involves groups of people. This can help them overcome a fear of men and children that inclines these people to avoid them. Working with organizations allows these people to be involved with many and this can be an aid in overcoming a lack of confidence in this area. Health problems involve the upper back, sides, heart, and the other areas ruled by this sign.

Virgo

These people have a fear of health problems. This is a difficult sign placement as these people could have a hard time with health in general, and many feel ill at numerous times during the day and night. They would do well to work with those who are ill, as it can alleviate worries over their own health problems which may be only trivial. There is a worry over trivia, and they should be guided toward the positive and serving side of the nature. This position is also related to work, which they have a tendency to overdo, or it can be one who simply does not wish to work.

Libra

These are individuals who experience difficulty in overcoming the fear of partners but who constantly search for the ideal partner. They will never find the partner that is up to their standards if they allow themselves to be influenced by the negative side of this placement. Their subconscious is searching for a lesser partner, but their conscious mind places such high standards they are unable to find the one they seek. Working with the public can help to overcome this obsession. Establishing a foundation for their leadership abilities could also help these persons overcome their fear. This is a difficult position for health because these people are unable to find true harmony within. The system is not properly balanced as the entire vaso-motor system of the body is affected. This is not the best placement to find harmony within oneself.

Scorpio

This causes problems with sexual relationships in youth that are generally overcome later in life as these people become more open-minded about such matters. These are often people who fear sex, and therefore could become an advocate of certain religious dogmas covering moral issues. Many also fear occult groups as well as the underworld and are therefore not inclined to join such organizations. They fear death and all matters relating to the sign. To overcome the fear, they should be guided to work in the area of the occult, which would lessen the obsession for money and material possessions.

Sagittarius

This is a sad placement because these people truly seeks spiritual guidance but do not have the confidence to stand up for any particular idealogy. This would indicate a bad philosopher if not used correctly. They constantly search for the spiritual but have difficulty finding what they perceive to be the truth. These people will be rewarded at a later time for no matter where Sagittarius is located in the chart, it will ultimately bring good to the individual. This is a good placement for working with spiritual affairs and teaching others what they have learned about philosophy and spirituality.

Capricorn

This is an interesting placement for it is the person who fears poverty and therefore constantly seeks to keep from being poor. It indicates those who work for others that are less fortunate than themselves, as they have an affinity for the mother figure and constantly look for someone to mother. The best people to mother are the less fortunate. They are not as concerned about their career as they are over what they are involved with, and their involvements do not generally encompass their career unless there is a strong placement to indicate otherwise.

Aquarius

These people believe in the standards of the past and therefore have little confidence in science and progress. They fear their friends because they feel that their friends may outdo them. These individuals should be guided to work with astrology, science, mechanics, and the other areas of this sign as they will ultimately find that they have a great aptitude for such affairs. There is always genius involved with the sign Aquarius.

Pisces

These people fear all the areas associated with this sign, such as hospitals, drugs, alcohol, and prisons. They would excel at working in a hospital as it would allow the service side of their nature to come forth; they make excellent healers. Seldom do they become drug addicts or alcoholics as they tend to stay away from these areas. Illness is less dramatic here than in its opposite sign Virgo. There would be some problems with the feet and some problems with disease, but this placement draws its health from Virgo, which enhances the general health.

"In the name of the Father, the Son, and the Holy Ghost, I come in the name of the Lord. What is important is not to be loved but to love. It is in the giving completely from the heart; the gift of yourself in helping others to find

the pure light. In this manner of service, you may truly receive the blessings of the soul from God. "—Spirit of Sister Ann

* * * * *

"Think not that thee will be in immortal danger. Thy Father would never allow more burdens than thee can bear. Through thine own free will thou mayest add to suffering, but this comes through thine own faults, not from thy Father in heaven. Therefore, it is truly written, 'Seek ye first the Kingdom of Heaven, and all things shall be open unto you.'"—Spirit of Father Malachai

Chapter 12

South Node in the Houses

First House

This placement can be difficult for the development of psychic awareness. These people are given the gift of spiritual development in the next plane of existence, and therefore it is best for them to work with others who have psychic ability and who have dedicated themselves to developing their psychic gifts. In this manner those with this configuration would learn lessons of the spiritual plane even though they are not personally receiving psychic messages. There is also difficulty in beginning anything new. There are always problems connected with starting things, which will continue throughout the lifetime. Many of the difficulties are tied up with the mind and in their way of thinking.

Second House

This is a poor placememnt for financial affairs and material possessions, and becomes a lifetime complaint with the individual. They often complain about their financial situation to others. This position is a blessing if these individuals choose to read this position in this way by forgetting their dependency on material possessions and financial wealth. They will find relief from this burden at another time and in another plane of existence. These persons are not totally deprived of money and possessions in every case, but will always feel they are lacking in enough of what they feel they need. They could very well be broke and dissatisfied with what they have, but will learn a very valuable lesson in suffering the lack of material wealth. These people learn to place more value on other matters. Even if they are involved in financial affairs, they can be dissatisfied with their existence, primarily because they are involved with money and material wealth. Difficulty with development of psychic gifts leads to difficulty with their creative processes. There is always a hindrance with creative pursuits.

Third House

There is a lack of confidence in communication abilities and difficulty in communicating with others. They are writers if they are pushed to be writers, for they have the gift of writing when they learn to use it properly. This can also be the individuals who cannot write at all because they refuse to write. It is difficult for psychic writing, especially if it is placed in a strong communication sign. It does, however, drive them to develop this placement, and those who have learned to use this placement wisely develop much faster on the long road of eternal life.

Fourth House

There are many problems for those who are involved with domestic life. These are the people who fling themselves into home life and other matters of this house, and become upset because of a lack of proficiency in this area. They strive to develop this placement, but have great difficulty in acquiring what they seek. They are constantly emotional regarding those things related to the sign and house placement. This position deprives the individual of a dominant parent or family, whether it be physical or mental, and causes problems with women. They are continually involved with Moon-type affairs, creating a sensitive reaction to women, which could include the mother of the individual.

Fifth House

This placement is difficult for communication with children, and indicates fear of children and others who do not totally accept their way of thinking. They are not likely to have children, but will be inclined to do so when they are working in this area. Negatively, these persons can shun their children, thus causing harm not only to themselves but to the child. This position can also bring about a difficult child, thereby causing problems in communication. No matter from what direction it comes, difficulty can be expected with all matters of this house, such as love, romance and speculation. These people should be very careful when engaged in speculation of any kind and when involved in the other areas related to this house.

Sixth House

These people have a tendency to be very critical, especially involving health and work. Negatively, this can be a hypochondriac, but when used in a positive manner, it can be a great healer. They must learn to overcome their lack of confidence in the matters of this house, for when this has been accomplished, these people can perform great things and be rewarded in many ways. If this placement is not overcome, the individual is lazy and does not want to work, or frequently changes jobs. Some do not enjoy their work and thus remain unhappy throughout their life.

Seventh House

This position can be a problem for anyone who expects to be married for any length of time as these individuals seek the ideal mate and never find what they are searching for. They can overcome this position by learning to live with a partner through elimination of the fear of marriage. If it takes staying married to eliminate the fear, then this is what the individual should do. These people can be easily persuaded to get married, but once they become slightly dissatisfied with the relationship, they end it. This is a good position for learning to work with the public. Great gains can be made if these people overcome their inhibitions about the world in general. They are afraid of the outside world and do their best to avoid public confrontation. Public contact would be very good for them, and the more involvement with the public, the better, even if it includes politics.

Eighth House

This placement brings out deception and ill-will when used negatively. These individuals should learn to overcome this by working for the benefit of others rather than concentrating on their own selfish interests. They learn many lessons with respect to the affairs of the dead and all those matters relating to the occult whether they wish to or not, and are continually involved in these areas in some way. It can be one who is a protagonist, or one who is an antagonist of the occult. Either way, it does not matter, because they will be involved with the affairs of the dead in one way or the other. There can be great difficulty with sex, or they can experience great sex, depending upon how they choose to overcome their particular incarnation. These people lack confidence with respect to sexuality, especially in the early years of his life; but the fear can be overcome.

Ninth House

This can bring sadness if not overcome as this is the house of God's spirituality. These people have chosen to overcome this particular obstacle for a very rewarding reason, and they can learn to develop their spirituality beyond belief in the next existence if they are not successful in this life. These people suffer much soul frustration as well as spiritual frustration, as the soul is the likeness of God that is given to each individual being. It would be wise for these people to develop spiritual awareness. They have difficulty accepting the chosen beliefs of their society and the philosophical beliefs of others, and should learn to overcome their inhibitions by searching out these areas because understanding of the spiritual negates fear. There should never be a fear of the spiritual. The lack of confidence extends to higher education, which is ruled by this house, and many of these people feel they do not have the ability to accomplish such a goal in this lifetime. If they commit themselves to higher education, their achievements would be beyond their wildest dreams.

Tenth House

This can be very difficult for those who desire a profound career because they just do not have the drive it takes to accomplish it in this lifetime. They continually complain about their misfortunes, and about that which they have not been given in this life. They are the poverty-oriented individuals who have a fear of poverty. This could drive them to work toward a goal of acceptance by the public in order that they could live their life out of poverty as they do not want to be classified as poor. These are people who work for the less fortunate if the opportunity to do so presents itself, and they can overcome their own fear of poverty by channeling it in a constructive way through helping others to make a better life for themselves. Those born into a wealthy family who have this placement are the individuals who are unhappy with their chosen field, or inclined to change fields frequently because they have chosen wrongly.

Eleventh House

This placement indicates a feeling that they are searching for the wrong goals in life, but what these people really desire is instant fame. They could be scientifically inclined, for example, but lack confidence in their ability to pursue this field. This placement brings difficulties with friendship by giving these individuals the feeling that their friends are not what they appear to be. This can be associated with those who work for an organization simply to work in it, even though the goals of the organization are not in line with what they feel they should be. However, this position can be used constructively if these individuals allow themselves to be more oriented to the views of others and less to their own views. Thus they will learn from others that their own views and opinions are not as detrimental as they felt they were.

Twelfth House

This indicates a fear of almost everything, especially those areas related to the house. There is a fear of hospitals, and the person tries to avoid them even at the expense of health. They should learn to work with those who are associated with hospitals and the other areas related to this house, thereby learning to cope with these fears.

They fear their own undoing, and can become puritannical in nature as they work to avoid it. A good example is the minister who preaches against all the pleasures of life. It can be associated with those who have such a fear of imprisonment that they never break a rule or law. On the other hand, it can be those who propel themselves toward criminal activity in spite of their fear of it.

Chapter 13

South Node Conjunct the Planets

Moon

This denotes changeability in areas ruled by the sign and house placement. These people experience changeable health conditions, and are prone to many ailments relating to the parts of the body ruled by the sign; they can become quite emotional over this. There is a tendency to criticize women, and these people can be uncomfortable around them. Criticism can extend to those persons who are of the sign of the conjunction.

Mercury

A confusing configuration, these individuals worry about those things ruled by the sign and is not in the proper frame of mind with respect to these areas. Worry extends to communication and problems connected with it, but any difficulty is in reality only mental. There can be some difficulty with the lungs, especially if the conjunction is in Gemini.

Venus

There is a lack of beauty, which may be physical or internal. They cause themselves to be less sociable in those particular places ruled by the sign and house. There is frustration over material possessions which they feel they lack or do not have in a sufficient amount.

Sun

There is a rejuvenating process here related to the sign of the conjunction that comes through the ego, for the ego would continually try to encourage them to overcome their lack of those things related to the sign placement. They hide their true feelings with respect to the sign placement, and these individuals feel they lack vitality, when in reality, their lack of vitality is only mental. This position is a blessing because it enables them to overcome any health problems they may encounter.

Mars

Here is an interesting configuration for the affect is to hold down the temperment of the person as indicated by the sign placement. This gives them the energy to go right to the source of a problem. It motivates them by giving them a little extra push to overcome a lack of confidence or health problem related to the sign. Unless there is a poor aspect to this conjunction by a strong planet, there would be only minor accidents rather than major ones. There could be trouble with sexual ability.

Saturn

This placement is for the best interests of the persons involved with it. A trying configuration, it indicates increased problems related to the sign placement. There is less ability to recover from illesses, but these people have the ability to overcome such obstacles. This is because they begin the incarnation with a strong health chart and have a strong source to draw from to help them endure this placement. Other sorrows befall them in connection with the sign and house placement, but the strength and ability are there to help them overcome the trials.

Jupiter

The benefits of Jupiter allow these people to overcome illness and lack of confidence related to the sign. However, they are weak-willed and need the influence of the great benefic, Jupiter, to help them overcome the obstacles chosen before birth. Although their financial situation could be weak in the sign area, it would not necessarily be weak throughout the chart, so they are not totally deprived of benefits that Jupiter can bring. For example, in the fourth house, they may lack sufficient money to fulfill every wish for the home, but still receive benefits for the home. Otherwise they would lack many of the necessities essential to life.

Uranus

There is an up and down movement with matters related to the sign placement. Emotionally, they would be up one day and down the next, especially if the conjunction is in an emotional sign. There is a benefit here in that it helps to direct the individual away from or toward the areas they should or should not be exposed to. They draw from the characteristics of the sign placement, which helps them to appropriately direct their lives. This also can be beneficial in health as they can be directed to the correct person or place in order to resolve a problem.

Neptune

This manifests as an incurable and irritating disease related to the sign of the conjunction unless there is a powerful, beneficial configuration to help pull the person out of this placement. An incurable disease could be one the person chose prior to incarnation in order to help elevate the soul. The disease may be devious, bringing much sorrow and suffering. This is the best placement for soul elevation if the person can endure it without resorting to suicide or bodily harm. These people may not necessarily die of the disease unless this placement is in opposition or conjunction to Saturn. The incurable illness can come later in the life if the chart points this way. This configuration does bring inspiration so that they can inspire others by showing the courageous side of their life.

Pluto

This is a very powerful configuration as these people are strong and have the ability to endure the life they have chosen to lead. Others are inspired by them. Pluto helps them overcome the obstacles of the South Node. These individuals incline toward being weak-willed and need this powerful planet to help them with their South Node placement. This placement is also given to strong-willed persons in order to enable them to overcome much hardship and the many obstacles they have chosen for this lifetime. This also can bring about a difficult transformation unless the individual uses the placement wisely.

Vulcan

This is good for healing when used with the opposite Node. These individuals are the hypochondriacs and the complainers when this placement is used negatively. The planets Saturn and Uranus in good aspect can help to pull the individual out of the negativity.

Persephone

It would be very good for these individuals to work with the North Node as it would bring out their creativity and endow them with a very cheery nature. They would be helpful to others through the use of their inspiring emotions. Since this planet is always good, it cannot be used negatively; however, when used improperly, there is a lack of confidence that can suppress creative abilities.

Chapter 14

South Node Conjunct Saturn in the Signs

The best advice that can be given to anyone with the South Node conjunct Saturn is to overcome the difficulties of Saturn by looking to the gift that God has given them: the North Node. People with this configuration will find that the North Node becomes an even greater gift for it will compensate them for the difficult lessons they are attempting to learn. All is well when there is faith in God, and any obstacle can be overcome when the placements are used properly.

Aries

This denotes difficulties and fear with beginnings. These people can learn to overcome fear by working with Saturn, and they should seek older persons in a setting that would be conducive to helping them with the public. If the individual learns to be a constructive leader, it brings many responsibilities and enhances development of psychic awareness. It can mean a hard young life, but a rewarding older life.

Taurus

There is an affinity for the occult with this placement, and if used in this way, these people can overcome many of the obstacles of this position. They would do well working with the occult and thus applying the benefits that Saturn brings through helping those less fortunate through the use of their psychic gifts. When this placement is used improperly, it brings difficulties with finances and problems with the throat and thyroid. If this placement is well aspected to the greater planets, they can overcome their financial burdens for the most part.

Gemini

This brings difficulties with relatives, and there could be a loss of someone related to the individual. They can become great teachers by working with older persons or the less fortunate, thereby developing great teaching ability rather than fear. There are difficulties with the communication process, but this can be overcome by working with Saturn. The gifts of Saturn are great if one learns to work with it, for this planet is the greatest of all teachers, and what better place to have this great teacher than in the sign of teaching.

Cancer

There are problems with the mother figure, and these people can eliminate their frustrations by working with the less fortunate, the poor, and older persons. This helps to cover up their own insecurity. These people enjoy working with these kinds of people, and by working with them, they can overcome their own difficulties. There are some problems with women, but this placement does not totally deny them communication or flexibility with women.

Leo

These people encounter problem children throughout the lifetime, and it is in their best interest to work with problem children in order to elevate their souls. They can work with organizations involved with problem children, but they must work with this placement or they will pay a penalty for ignoring that which God has given them to do. They know the best avenue to direct their energies as they have been given the wisdom and knowhow to help the unfortunate and young souls who are lost.

Virgo

This denotes difficulties in the area of employment and health. Relief can be obtained by working with the opposite placement. These are the spiritual people who work to serve others, and by working with the North Node placement they are relieved of the suffering they encounter. They have a choice to work with this placement or ignore it. If it is ignored, they will continue to have difficulties with their health and employment. If they learn to work with it, their problems will be almost completely eliminated.

Libra

Problems concerning the public can be overcome if these individuals bring their leadership ability to the public. They have been given a good mind to bring this about. When they learn to use the mind to help guide other people, the difficulties encountered with the public will be overcome. This position indicates problems with partners, but the difficulties are only temporary, depending upon other aspects.

Scorpio

This represents difficulties with sex and the occult. By incorporating the opposite nodal placement, they can overcome the fear of these things through the gift of love from Venus. There can be difficulty with the occult, but when these individuals reach an older age, they can become very good psychics. These people can help older persons with their sex life, as well as the less fortunate. They are given the gift of love, which is God's greatest gift of all.

Sagittarius

Here is the doubtful philosopher. They doubt what they hear about the spiritual and the philosophical. By working with the opposite nodal placement and overcoming their fear of the spiritual, they can become great spiritual teachers. They would do well to pursue this goal. When older, they will be able to grasp the meaning of true spirituality.

Capricorn

This brings trouble with older persons and finances. This is due to difficulty with the career which brings problems to their earning ability. These persons should choose a career that enables them to work with women which would help them to overcome their fears with respect to their profession. They can relate to women far better than the average person. This can bring leadership ability when used properly as it is a responsible position.

Aquarius

This brings difficulties with friends. However, by working with their opposite placement, the fear of people is overcome. They do have an affinity for older and less fortunate people as they feel they are the only people they can trust as friends. Their friends will seek them out, thus bringing on difficulties. These people love children, but they have to learn to love their friends.

Pisces

There can be a great fear of the unknown with this configuration as well as problems with alcohol and drugs. These people should avoid taking alcohol and drugs, as it can be detrimental, and instead work with a health organization. These individuals should use their psychic ability for the benefit of older persons. They would have less fear of the psychic when they are involved with more mature persons they feel they can trust. These are the people who become better psychics later in life after they learn to overcome the obstacle of fear. This placement can indicate a more sensitive nature. They should throw themselves into their work and forget their difficulties, which pass with age.

> *"There are things more important for the progression of your souls than happiness. But without joy in your hearts, you could not fully appreciate the blessings bestowed upon you.*

> *"The Father always watches over his children, and the children feel safe if they accept the Father's love and let it surround and protect with this love. Toy will always remain in your hearts with love from the Father.*

> *"Mayall your days be filled with sunshine even when it rains, for this is what creates the rainbows."*—The Spirit of Joy

Chapter 15

South Node Conjunct Uranus in the Signs

Aries

This is difficult for leadership and beginnings as these people are learning to live with unusual activities related to both. They are erratic when dealing with matters ruled by this sign. Overcoming these obstacles depends upon the use the individual makes of the opposite nodal placement. One with leadership ability should look to Uranus to overcome the obstacles of the South Node.

Taurus

There are problems with financial affairs and earning ability as these people will always have an unusual way of earning money. This denotes those who work hard for material gain but who ultimately lose it in some manner. They should try to overcome the urgency to obtain material possessions since the lesson they must learn is that of unexpected problems with their earning ability. No matter how hard they work to make money, something unusual will come along to take it away. They are erratic with their own spending habits, spending their money on unusual things.

Gemini

These people have unusual writmg and communication abilities. They write erratically and learn their lessons in the same manner. They have difficulty learning to communicate from an early age. They write with an erratic hand movement in addition to communicating in an unusual manner from a mental standpoint. They should look to their North Node placement to control these tendencies.

Cancer

This denotes an unusual home life for women within the influence of these people. They should avoid contact with women who are promiscuous or inclined to be less domestic, and they tend to gravitate toward the lower type of female. These individuals feel that the home is an unusual place and they constantly seek enjoyment elsewhere. It is their unusual lifestyle that results in their unhappiness.

Leo

This indicates unusual childhood development as well as unusual children. They should try to work with less fortunate children for they do have an understanding of these problems. There are unusual relationships with men and love affairs. However, men and love affairs can become less important as the needs of children are greater than the needs of adults.

Virgo

There are unusual health and work problems throughout the lifetime. They are inclined toward fad diets and unusual eating habits. These people can be led into improper diets by people who really do not care whether the diet is good for them, and since they are attracted to unusual diet and health plans, they should be very cautious in health-related areas.

Libra

This placement brings an unusual partner to these individuals. There is also an erratic relationship with others, and an unusual outlook on the public. Their opposite nodal placement, when worked with properly, will bring unusual leadership abilities with the public and can help them to perceive public opinion differently. They perceive the public in an unusual way but have a great influence upon the community in some way. Therefore, they should be careful as to how they use their North Node placement. They have the ability to lead, but their leadership ability can be unusual because of the influence of public opinion, and they do not correctly perceive the public or public opinion. By working with astrology and the planet Uranus, they can overcome their unusual views.

Scorpio

This denotes unusual sex partners, but the sex partners can also bring unusual sex hangups. The hangups can be related to health, such as the person having a fear of venereal diseases. These individuals can overcome these obstacles by looking to their creative outlets, which will thus encourage sexual creativity. By working with the opposite node of creativity and incorporating it with the sexual, they can learn to overcome their fear of sex. Creative outlets can be used within the framework of sexual therapy.

Sagittarius

Here is the unusual philosopher. These people bring unusual ideas to Eearth, and stir up the youth of the world with them. They are the teachers of the world, and should be careful about spreading their predictions and philosophy as it attracts others to their ideology. If this placement is not properly aspected, great harm can result through the spreading of untruths.

Capricorn

This brings unusual and unexpected troubles with older persons. These individuals will have an unusual older age, and before they pass into the spirit world, they will become involved with unusual activities. They would do well working with the aged while they are young as this can bring out their maternal urges and help to overcome much of the troubles that come later in life. Improperly used, they would have erratic career problems, but this placement should be aspected to the greater planets to determine whether it will be used improperly.

Aquarius

These individuals are scattered and concerned about these tendencies. They continually unsettle themselves over something or other, but this instability can be overcome to a large extent by working with the opposite Node. They find themselves in unusual places in life, and are always looking for the one person who will help them to overcome these obstacles. They should be encouraged to find a relationship with a stable individual who can help them to overcome their fear of becoming unduly scattered. These people are the great lovers of the universe for they love all. But they fear humanity and what humanity can do to all that they love.

Pisces

These people are fearful and they are unusual worriers. Some have anxiety attacks, and they should stay away from alcohol and drugs, as it can adversely affect them. These are the people whose ailments are misdiagnosed, so they should seek a second opionion before accepting treatment. Diet is extremely important here, and these individuals should be encouraged to eat properly and stay on a prescribed diet. They find themselves in unusual difficulties as they become involved with not only their own problems but with the problems of others. They do have unusual dreams that are prophetic, and if they would use this spiritual outlet, they will overcome their fears.

Chapter 16

South Node Conjunct Neptune in the Signs

Aries

Some of these people are weak of mind and thought, and prone to mental illness. It indicates one who wishes to work with the occult but would not understand that which is received. It can be the creative person, but the creative abilities are apt to be used improperly. However, if the individual allow creativity to flow forth naturally, it can be very beneficial.

Taurus

There can be deception in matters of money and financial affairs. They are jealous of others, and inclined to deception when involved with material things. There can therefore be problems with financial and material possessions. Working with the occult and the psychic can help to overcome deceptive behavior, as well as bring forth the creative side of their nature. In the area of health, this brings problems with the throat, thyroid and other parts of the body ruled by this sign.

Gemini

This is a devious placement that brings out the negative side of the personality. Working with the opposite Node can help to overcome this. These individuals would do well to stay away from things that are harmful to the lungs, and they have a tendency for smoking and other popular vices.

Cancer

This can be an indicator of one who easily deceives women, including the mother of the person. They would do well to work for organizations that unify the women of the world in orler to equalize their role in society. Tlese people become very emotional over Neptunian matters, but this can be overcome when used properly; that is, when the opposite Node is utilized. Women with this placement should check those areas relating to the female parts of the body as well at the other parts ruled by this sign that are applicable to both genders.

Leo

These people do well working with children as they are very good at inspiring them when the placement is properly used. They have an aptitude for such endeavors. They can be easily deceived by men but they can also deceive them. It is, therefore, better for them to work with children as it brings out the inspiring side of the nature. There is a tendency for heart problems and other ailments related to the sign.

Virgo

This inspires these people to work in the area of health, but since there is a tendency to drug abuse, they should avoid such fields where drugs are dispensed. It would also be advisable that they not work where alcoholic beverages are handled unless there are other strong indicators in the chart to the contrary. Diseases of this placement concern the lower intestines and colon areas.

Libra

These people are easily deceived by partners as well as the public. They cannot see things as they truly are. There is a fear of deception from the public, but by working with the opposite Node, this fear can be overcome. This would then give them a more outgoing personality. The affect of this placement on the body is in the lower back region and infections of the kidneys.

Scorpio

These individuals would do well in work for an investigative agency of the government. Some are involved in the underworld. They can be deceptive and secretive, and cause injury to others if this placement is not used in a positive manner. These people can be very negative persons when this conjunction is used improperly, and they can be easily lost in their own illusions of what death is, thereby becoming involved with it in a destructive manner. The sexual and rectal areas are affected by this placement and diseases can occur in these parts of the body.

Sagittarius

This indicates spiritual inspiration when the individuals have come to grips with what constitutes spirituality. Working with the opposite Node can bring out the positive side of the nature. A poor aspect to this conjunction, however, can indicate those who use God for their own greed and, through deception, cause great harm to many. These people have an aptitude for teaching, whether it be truth or untruth. They are susceptible to diseases of the blood, thereby causing problems with circulation as well as those parts of the body involved with the blood.

Capricorn

This is an unfortunate placement for governmental affairs, although there many with this configuration work for the government. It is good, however, for working with women in the government as this is considered a constructive use of this placement. They are susceptible to skin rashes and could have difficulties with the skin area and knees.

Aquarius

This is a poor placement for those who wish to work in a scientific field or astrology. There is a tendency to see things unrealistically. They do have creative minds, and would do well to work with children, or with organizations that involve both genders.

Organizational ability is good. There can be problems with the circulation and they should be careful to always eat properly and have regular checkups of their circulatory system. It is advisable that they limit salt.

Pisces

Improperly used, this can indicate an extremely deceptive individual. When used properly, it can be the creative artist or psychic. They should avoid drugs, alcohol, and other habit-forming activities. These people are influenced by deceptive individuals. Much of this can be avoided if they are engaged in working with the less fortunate or in a service industry. A trine to Saturn is a positive indication.

Chapter 17

South Node Conjunct Pluto in the Signs

The South Node is beneficial if appropriately used, and those with the South Node conjunction Pluto should learn to live and to love this placement for they are the ones who can truly understand it; it will be very significant in their life. The transits of Pluto will have much influence on them, and they will be rewarded for learning to work with it by being given the gift of Light, which is for all to understand and to hold in their hearts. There are rewards of the universe to be had when Pluto gives them the universe to rule. The mysteries of Pluto have yet to be uncovered, but this will happen one day in order to facilitate the development of Earth.

Aries

This is a strong placement for initiative and gives these people many new starts in life. It bestows great leadership ability for they are born leaders. They have been given the gift of leadership for the purpose of developing others psychically and spiritually, and this placement is good for almost anything that requires strong leadership ability.

Best House Position: The seventh house is the best for initiating those things related to the public, as well as the partner. The third house is equally as good because the person would initiate communications involving this psychic gift.

Taurus

Great strength is given to the individuals with this configuration. They are given great beauty relating to the house, such as the first house, where there would be great strength related to mental activities and learning. It gives beautiful thinking or beautiful features of the head area, such as the hair, face, or mind. Although it is not a good placement for beauty if poorly aspected, it would still give a good ability to understand beauty. These people are creative and productive in those things ruled by this sign.

Best House Position: The eighth house gives the person ability to do good things with other people's money, and would thus be a good banker or one who works with money.

Gemini

These people have a natural gift for communication, writing, and speaking. They have a great influence over relatives and can be domineering and possessive of them. They should be directed toward developing their psychic gift of writing, which would be easy for them.

Best House Position: The fifth house is the best position as they would be good at writing plays, and it would bring a great love to the Gemini who has a hard time finding love on a permanent basis.

Cancer

There is great spiritual strength relating to matters of the home and women. These people are very emotional and sensitive to matters of the psychic world. However, they should not develop their psychic gifts as their emotional feelings enter into their spiritual development. They are sensitive to women but not necessarily to the mother, as the mother can have the tendency to tear down the home life of those with this placement.

Best House Position: The second house of possessions is a placement where these people can become emotionally involved. By doing this, they reduce their sensitivity to other people. Obviously, the seventh house would be the worst position. These are extremely sensitive persons no matter where this is located in the chart.

Leo

This is a good placement because it indicates a great love and a big heart. These people have a heart of gold and are concerned about the welfare of children and loved ones. They are the lovers of the universe, and the ones who share their winnings (they have the ability to be winners). Because they have the strength of Pluto and the love of God to draw from, they are here to benefit all.

Best House Position: The eleventh house of humanity is the best position. Who else would wish their friends love but Pluto in Leo?

Virgo

This is a good placement for healing and helping others, so an oustanding physician might have this configuration. They are hard workers in whatever field they are in, here to help others who are less fortunate because these people have been given the strength of Pluto to help and heal others. They are the healers of the universe.

Best House Position: The first and seventh houses are both good for this placement. The first house of the head is good for psychic healers, and the seventh house of the public indicates the ability to help many.

Libra

These people help society because they are fair and just individuals. They have been given this in order to help balance the universe because the Earth will be in turmoil when they mature. They are the lawyers and practical helpers of the Earth plane, and will help form a new justice that come with the Age of Aquarius. They will help those who will need the comfort of balance after turmoil on Earth.

Best House Position: The seventh house is the best position because they can help all of society.

Scorpio

This is a good placement for the occult and for the development of the underworld. These people are very much concerned with their sex lives, but when this concern is overcome, they lean more toward spiritual development. This can be the Eagle or the Scorpion. A positive aspect would help bring out the better side of this sign. It is a very powerfui configuration for it brings the rower of Pluto as well as the traits of Scorpio, but these people should be very careful when dealing with the underworld. They have an investigative nature, but not necessarily the best investigative minds, and must learn to overcome the negative side of their nature as they are tempted to use this power deceptively.

Best House Position: The best house position is the ninth as it can assist in bringing out the spiritual side of this configuration, thus helping to counter the balance that needs to be maintained.

Sagittarius

This is a spiritual configuration and one that is very beneficial to others. These people are good at inspiring others, both spiritually and sexually. They are lovers in the game of playmates, and their athletic ability should be used to its fullest because it helps to stimulate the spiritual side of their development. This is beneficial to those interested in helping the handicapped. When used spiritually, these persons make great teachers.

Best House Position: The best houses are the fifth and sixth. Both would be very good for bringing love and service to others.

Capricorn

The true farmers of the coming age will have this configuration. They will be excellent in working with their hands in replanting the earth for future generations. Their farming abilities, literally and figuratively, will be their strength. These people are good to have around for guidance on governmental issues as they have a natural gift for understanding the system of government. They will be here when the Earth will need them the most, and the Earth will appreciate their loving hands.

Best House Position: The best house position is the fourth, as it will enable these people to have the understanding of the land as well as the ability to work it.

Aquarius

This is an unhappy position as the psychic gifts are scattered. Although this is the sign of the genius, it is only for a particular purpose, which these people must find. They are great humanitarians and astrologers, but they will be unable to use the gift of astrology to its fullest potential. This is because they will not have the needed tools and their gift will be only be seen as useful only during the times of harvesting and planting. The Capricorn influence will override the astrological influence, although these persons will be gifted, their gift will be almost useless.

Best House Position: The best position is the tenth house, which will be very beneficial to those who are tilling the soil.

Pisces

These people are dreamers, but also great healers of those less fortunate than themselves. They are best able to understand their spiritual gifts, and to direct this toward helping the less fortunate because they connect with the sorrows of others. If this placement is used negatively, it is associated with people who are just dreamers. Used positively, it indicates those who are the healers of the less fortunate.

Best House Position: The best position is the fourth house, which gives these people the stability they otherwise would lack. It gives them a feeling of security.

Chapter 18

South Node Conjunct Lilith in the Signs

This brings difficulties that plague the individuals throughout the lifetime. The rewards for those who have this placement will be realized later in the life because its effects lessen with time. The interpretations for this conjunction apply to both the natal and solar return charts.

The lessons of the South Node conjunct Lilith can only be truly understood by those who have this placement. The internal frustration is much greater than one can imagine as these persons have been deprived of one of God's blessings. This is something they will truly realize this at some point in their life.

Aries

There are difficulties in the early life, and they have ongoing difficulty in starting anything new, as well as overcoming the South Node placement. These people should work with both the South Node and North Node even though they may be unable to overcome the obstacles they will encounter. There are problems connected with the head region and with other areas related to the sign placement, such as with leadership ability. This is an extremely difficult placement, but these people will accomplish much by working with the Nodes.

Taurus

This brings ongoing problems with finances, and these people have a difficult, albeit active, social life. Some of the difficulties can be overcome through the North Node placement of the occult and spiritual, which can help to alleviate much of the tension in their lifetime. This is the best outlet for these people, as the Lilith deprives. There can be difficulties with the throat and thyroid area, and thus they should pay attention to these areas of the body.

Gemini

There are communication difficulties with relatives, as well as strained relations. At the least, there can be less of a relationship than these people would like to have. There can be a health problem related to the lungs or appendages. By using their North Node placement in the sign of the spiritual, these problems can be eliminated.

Cancer

This denotes difficulties with the home, real estate, and women. These people are deprived of an influential mother figure, which can be difficult because it also deprives the person of a true beginning and a true home life. These people can benefit from using their North Node placement even though it would not entirely alleviate the problem. Working with the less fortunate can help to compensate for a difficult childhood.

Leo

These people are deprived of a true love as well as children, and this placement brings difficulties with children in addition to some form of deprivation. They should work with organizations rather than individuals as this would help to overcome their lack of a true love or romantic relationship. In other words, the person would do best working with groups rather than to look for the love of their life.

Virgo

This placement indicates continual health problems throughout the lifetime. They can benefit from working in hospitals as this would give them access to the things they need to help their own health. There is also difficulty with employment and employees. Much of the tension encountered can be relieved through working with the North Node placement.

Libra

Problems are associated with the creative abilities of these individuals, and with finding a true partner in this lifetime. This position stifles creative processes, and also indicates a fear of the public as well as a loss in some way tied to the public. To counteract this, they should be involved with the opposite sign placement, Aries.

Scorpio

This affects the psychic abilities unless there is another indication in the chart to the contrary. These people are paying for what was done by them in a prior life, and they are thus being suppressed in an important gift—that of the psychic. They must work doubly hard to experience the benefits that the Nodes can bring. There is difficulty with the sex life, as well as health problems connected with sex. They will criticize the occult world and the underworld. Unless there are strong indications to the contrary, they would benefit from working with the creative as indicated by the North Node position.

Sagittarius

People with this placement have difficulties with the spiritual. They are working on a past experience where they were overly pious and are compensating for this by being deprived of the spiritual in this life. These people can benefit from becoming well educated or by working with the North Node in some form or manner. They will always have difficulty accepting or believing anything spiritual, although the spiritual is there for the asking. In the area of health, there can be difficulties with the blood in some way.

Capricorn

This brings poverty in some form, and it indicates the less fortunate individual. These people will be involved with the poor or poverty in some way, whether they are in this situation through their career or were born to a poor family. This placement indicates some difficulties with the career. In health, they can experience problems with the knees or the other parts of the body ruled by this sign.

Aquarius

These individuals have difficulty with the scientific and the spiritual. It is also difficult for them when dealing with astrology and other areas ruled by this sign. They should work for humanity by working with children as this will help to compensate for the frustrations within and give them an outlet to express their emotional needs. There are circulatory problems connected with this configuration so they should pay attention to this area.

Pisces

This is an unfortunate configuration in that these people will experience continual bouts with disease and infection. There are difficulties with the feet area as well as spiritual development. Working with the North Node in the sign of health will help to compensate for some of the problems encountered. This placement can bring sorrow through suffering, and if they work for others who are less fortunate, it will help to lessen their suffering. This position can become even more difficult because these individuals can be very much in love with themselves and therefore have trouble compensating for their feelings. They often feel sorry for themselves as they enjoy worrying and have much to worry about. This is a difficult position, but with the help of God, all things are possible. This position will always be trying and difficult for these people to overcome because they have been given a lesson to learn and therefore some of the blessings have been taken away.

> *"My children, my children. Have mercy. I weep for my foolish children. Have mercy upon them most merciful Father. The burdens are great. We understand so little until it is too late. Pray for us now, and at the hour of our death, and for the times of our future lives. It grieves us when you will not listen and shut us out."*—The Spirit of the Keeper of the Children (Received during the Tones massacre at Guiana.)

* * * * *

> *"There are many hardships that must be faced by each individual. Do not be discouraged as there are rewards to come from every burden that is born. There are earthly rewards as well as heavenly rewards. There are times that the mundane problems seem so great that there is difficulty in be-*

lieving that the Father is there giving his love and protection. This is a hardship that is experienced by every individual at one time or another. Often it is not easy for one in the physical body to have complete faith in the Father above.

"We are here to help ease the gap between yourselves and the Father. We know your every thought and we help you to regain faith by putting the thoughts in your minds that this is a time that must be looked on as a growth period.

"Keep the faith in the Father, and you will find the burdens easier to bear."—Spirit of Paddy

Chapter 19

Transiting Planets Conjunct
the Natal South Node

Moon

The effect of the Moon transiting the South Node is minimal because the transit is so short that the individual hardly notices it. This transit would elevate the emotions for a brief period and cause a change of mind or attitude. There is only a brief effect with this transit.

Sun

This replenishes the vitality for the Sun is the giver of life and therefore gives the individual a certain amount of energy. The person can exhibit quite a bit of exuberance during this transit.

Mars

The influence of Mars can bring a particularly large amount of energy to the individual, or it may bring a problem. The sign involved in the conjunction is important as this transit can be influenced by the transit of another planet. This is a good time to begin new projects or restart those that were postponed. With Mars there is always a way out, so it does not necessarily mean there will be a harmful effect. These people should begin to work in an area they have been avoiding, or have tried to avoid.

Jupiter

This planet influences the natal South Node in a beneficial manner. There is a spiritual influence brought by Jupiter, and also material benefits; however, the important influence is that of the spiritual. This transit is the message that God wishes to give the individual and it is done by sending Jupiter to conjunct the natal South Node. It brings a spiritual understanding to a great many people if the conjunction is in a public sign or house. It has a great effect upon each individual by bringing spiritual awareness, material benefits, or great happiness.

Saturn

This is the opposite of the Jupiter transit as it brings sorrow to the individual. The influence of Saturn is great and this brings a devastating experience that is remembered for a long time. The individual will experience a loss or grievance of some kind that is associated with the sign and house placement. For example, in Virgo in the fifth house, there could be the loss of a loved one due to a health problem, or the loss of a child. This may not be death, but there would be a loss of some kind. This can also involve the loss of a job or aggravate an existing illness. In addition, it could bring back an old illness that has been dormant for a while because Saturn always digs up what is there. The sign and house are the indicators of the type of loss or sorrow the person will experience.

Uranus

This is the planet that is the most influential in the chart, and is present when the time comes for a change in the person's life. This transit creates severe changes for the individual, even in a fixed sign. The person is changeable and erratic for the entire period of the transit, with the most erratic change occurring when the transit is close by degree. In Taurus, for example, it would denote severe changes in the area of money and possessions, and it would be difficult for such a fixed and stubborn sign. The influence of Uranus upon the South Node is great and very severe.

Neptune

This is an interesting transit as it is often deceptive. People are unaware of changes taking place in their thinking, although the changes occur for only a brief period despite the long transit of Neptune through a sign (fourteen years). The influence of Neptune is illusive and deceptive, and with this transit approaching, people should be aware that it brings stress related to a disease that occurs in an unusual manner. They are prone to disease at this time. The effect of the disease and the influence of Neptune is for only a brief period, as Neptune is weak when transiting the South Node. The influence is there in the chart, but is not so drastic that affected individuals will suffer for fourteen years with a particular disease. (This can happen, but is not probable.)

Pluto

This is a strange transit that denotes a severe change within the structure of the person as revealed by the sign and house. Pluto tears down and rebuilds, and these individuals must deal with it as it occurs. This is the cleansing and regenerative action of Pluto. It is for all to experience in some way but to never be totally understood, for this planet works in a mysterious way when affecting the individual.

The transits of all other planets to the South Node are minimal, and do not require interpretation. Venus, Mercury, Vulcan and Persephone would have only a very weak influence that would not be noticed.

> *"One's soul is not elevated when things are easy and when the path is smooth. It is when a person overcomes difficulties without bitterness that the soul is elevated.*
>
> *"Remember, that what appears to be a burden can truly be a blessing, and that which appears to be a blessing can become a burden. Taking the easy path—having an easy life—does not result in the elevation of the soul.*
>
> *"Why should anyone seek the spiritual if everything is going well, and their greatest concern is what they will wear; what they should buy, or which way they will spend their money. "*—Spirit of Orthocar

Chapter 20

Saturn-Uranus Conjunction in the Houses

First House

These individuals suffer a sudden and tragic loss during their early years. They will be tragically involved in something that will destroy or take away a relationship on which their life revolved. They will be greatly influenced by this occurrance from the beginning and throughout their entire lifespan. These people are unable to begin things or will do so for only a short period of time before ending in an unusual manner. They suffer much sorrow through this configuration for they have chosen to endure this throughout their lifetime.

Second House

With this position, possessions are not held for a long time. This lack is felt on an emotional level because for the most part they are only involved with possessions in this way. They retain possessions for a short time, and then an event will occur that will take them away. They suffer from the loss until they realize they were actually too involved with their possessions to begin with. This configuration can denote a bankruptcy, or an event that will influence material possessions for a certain length of time. This would be a poor configuration for a speculator, as a loss is certain with this placement.

Third House

This is a painful placement for those who truly enjoy communication as they are cut off from many related activities. They participate only briefly because then a sudden change occurs to alter their lives and they suffer the loss of time and devotion to a particular area that is greatly influencing their lives. Although at another time they will receive this gift, in this life they must learn to endure the lessons of the conjunction. Wherever this conjunction occurs, the genius of Uranus is robbed by Saturn. The ability to develop the genius is there, but it is ultimately denied in one way or another. For example, they can be very good writers but will encounter obstacles that alter their ability or prevent them from fulfilling their goals. They can be involved with relatives, but have a hard time expressing themselves to them and thus lose the closeness of the relationship.

Fourth House

These people are denied a true home life within this lifetime. They long for the time they lived in this very secure framework, but they are unable to reproduce this feeling in this life. They are lost without the foundation of home and family, and long for a security that is never fulfilled.

Fifth House

This placement brings much sorrow through children. Although these people love and care for children, they suffer a loss because of a particular child or children. They have chosen to have this placement in order to appreciate children more because in the past they were unaware of them and have chosen to develop the love and appreciation of a small child. This could have the same effect with a loved one, and could be a grievance over a departed loved one or a past relationship that was never consumated.

Sixth House

A difficult configuration, it shows much sorrow through an ailment that continuously plagues the individual. It may be a lifetime of unexpected suffering because of an illness contracted through work, such as coal miners and factory workers who suffer from lung cancer and other diseases. They wish to be of great service to mankind, but are denied the ability to serve because of obstacles in their way. They have the ability to stay at a particular job for a great length of time, and it is because of this that they develop a particular disease from the work they are doing. Otherwise, there would be many changes in employment.

Seventh House

This position indicates a lifetime of losing partners, and these people are continually dissatisfied with partner or lover. They are allowed to experience many partners so that they may truly appreciate the convenience of having one throughout life. They are the roamers of the marriage market. Although they are always dissatisfied with the chosen person, in reality they are really dissatisfied with themselves. They truly wish to be a good partner, but do not have the stamina it takes to be a faithful one. This may also apply to a business partnership, and these people would not be good in a business arrangement that constitutes a partnership.

Eighth House

This causes much frustration to one those with psychic ability. They can overcome the frustration in time because they truly wish to be in the service of God. However, they have chosen this difficult placement in order to appreciate the gift of spiritual communication. These people enjoy sexual pleasures but have difficulty expressing their emotions to others. They are not denied the pleasures of sex, but do become frustrated with their endeavors. They constantly place obstacles within the mind so that the frustration is difficult to overcome. These people should look to their communication abilities with the spiritual world rather than search for complete sexual fulfillment.

Ninth House

These individuals seek a spiritual existence but lose their direction even though they very much need spiritual guidance to stay on the proper course. Their hearts are in the right place but look for the spiritual in the wrong places. They will in a future life be the spiritual givers of God's love, but in this lifetime experience great difficulty communicating spiritual love to the world. These people develop a downtrodden spirit, but will be greatly rewarded for their suffering. They have the gift of the spiritual given them by God, but are denied the ability to present it to others. These are people who seek out the cults and other religions and philosophies that border on the truth, but which only obscure the true light of God.

Tenth House

This placement brings great frustration with government and career, and even if these people are gifted within this framework, they are denied their full potential. This is a difficult position for them to work out. It is also a karmic position in that the reincarnation they expect to have is denied. They become confused at their immediate passing, but work out of this confusion in time. These people benefit from overcoming such a difficult obstacle—that of passing in a confused rather than a stable state of existence.

Eleventh House

There are many changes within the lifetime of these people, and the changes are not as good as expected. Their hopes and wishes are denied, they look for results that do not materialize, and they hope for the best but instead get the worst. This is not a good position for exploration or gambling. At times they are at a loss for direction, but then a new direction suddenly occurs. This keeps these individuals in a turmoil. They have great aspirations for their friends, but can be misdirected by them. This would not necessarily be intentional on the part of their friends, but they can be considered the catalyst for the events that occur. They would like to join organizations, but learn at a very early age to stay clear of them.

Twelfth House

This is the house of sorrow and confinement, and these people are confined in one way or another, and not necessarily in a prison or another institution. These people can be those who are interested in the spiritual but have a difficult time finding their way through it. It can also be those who are confined to a particular type of religion or an event that influences their lifetime. They have a difficult time finding the proper direction to pursue the spiritual, and they become lost within their own confusion. Very often, women with this placement become nuns, and the men become monks, and then they find themselves frustrated by the commitment to such an obligation. These people are lost within their own illusive world, and thereby confine themselves to this existence. They try to find peace of mind through these areas because they believe they are doing God's work, but in reality are not. They will be rewarded with true spirituality after they pass into the next plane of existence.

"Do not forget thou are in the Neptunian age. The properties of the planet are changeable - from inspiration to deception, and then inspiration again. Therefore, thou canst pass judgment on that of good or evil, for they change with time.

"There has been misuse of astrology and religion, and this makes not good or bad but changeability, and man reflects the times. Think ye not that astrology is right and the church is wrong. They are tools used by man who is human and prone to error. The fault lies within thyselves if the tool is misused.

"Tis not the church or astrology which is good or evil, but the good or evil is the result of the use of the tools."—Spirit of Father Malachai

Appendix
Dealing with Emotions

"When individuals feel crowded by others, it is best that they remind themselves that all who live on the physical plane, as well as all other planes, have a direct bearing on each other. How they feel and how they deal with their feelings is how they grow.

"Everyone who makes contact with another has a definite purpose to fulfill at that point in time. Each one relates to another in some way. It is not always recognizable at the time of occurance. It is not always known even later in time for as it becomes further in the past, the memory is pushed so far into the subconscious that is is no longer readily available to the person or persons involved. Sometimes these experiences will be brought to the surface so as to help cope with another situation presently being experienced.

"Those who find themselves in situations which make them feel uncomfortable, often find that they become upset and irritable as a result. It is not necessarily so, for all have the ability within themselves to control their feelings. All that need be done is remain calm. It is not uncommon to feel upset and irritable. There are more who react in this manner than there are those who do not. Those who have this tendancy should be ever on guard to protect themselves from being caught up, so to speak, in the situation. It would be better for all involved if they would try to stay peaceful within themselves rather than looking at the situation as it appears on the outside. When individuals are capable of remaining calm under stressful type situations when they are accustomed to 'falling apart', they have accomplished a very important task in the journey through the physical plane. Persons often find it difficult to become practiced in this method of controlling feelings, but it is possible for everyone to accomplish this while remaining in the flesh.

"The next time you are exposed to a situation that makes you feel that you would rather run as far as you can to get away from it, try to remain calm on the inside. You will discover the situation will change its perspective. You will be happier with yourself, as well as those around you.

"Those that fear life and the situations that life presents, it is difficult to remain calm. Life should be considered a school. People are on the physical plane to learn to deal with emotions and to grow. Of course, there are those in the category of human beings who seem to be very well established emotionally, but there are more who are not emotionally equipped, so they think, to tend to the situations that life presents. When they find themselves repeatedly facing emotional type situations, they often feel they are being pushed around. Each situation occuring in one's life is presented for the purpose of growing. As they journey through the physical plane, they should grow in the ability to deal with emotional problems. They should not become discouraged with themselves, as this only makes it more difficult to master the difficult problems. This is like adding fuel to the fire. Being discouraged has kept more people from growing than is realized.

"We on the spiritual plane are forever striving to encourage our individuals from being lost and forlorn. We try to get them to not become depressed because they feel they have failed. Of course, this is very difficult for us to do. Those on the physical plane must be willing to accept the guidance provided. If this is refused, we on the spiritual plane have no choice but to stay out of it. We then proceed to help through prayer alone.

"This is the time in the era of time that people have little understanding of themselves due to constant outside pressures. These pressures are strengthened from within the individual. If people would become more in control of their feelings, they would be able to more readily and easily deal with their problems as they arise. Those with little awareness of the spiritual, find it even more difficult to cope with them. If we on the spiritual plane could only stress upon the minds of everyone how much help is available in times of need, our particular work would be much more easily accomplished. Those who shut out the recommendations of their spirit guides as to how to deal with everyday situations find themselves getting into deeper and deeper emotional problems. There are so many who have been lead astray by so many different sources that it is really most difficult for most spirit guides to get through to the individual they are guiding.

"Listen carefully to the voice within, and remember to remain calm!"—*The Spirit of Agnes*

www.ingramcontent.com/pod-product-compliance
Lightning Source LLC
LaVergne TN
LVHW061227060426

835509LV00012B/1454